A GRANDPARENTS BOOK

HPBooks

THOUGHTS, MEMORIES,
AND HOPES
FOR A GRANDCHILD

A GRAND-PARENTS' BOOK

PRODUCED BY JAMES WAGENVOORD

Created and produced by
James Wagenvoord Studio, Inc.

ISBN O-89586-151-8

HPBooks
Box 5367
Tucson, AZ 857O3
(6O2) 888-215O

Assisting in the creation of this book: Lorna Bieber,
Megan Marshack, Amelia Wood, Fiona St. Aubyn,
Anne Dodd, Marta Norman, Dewey Thompson,
Guthrie Sayen, Maurrie Brown.

Design: Ulrich Ruchti

Cover Design: Richard Nebiolo

Printed and manufactured in the United States of
America. Fourth Edition.

Contents

A Grandparents' Book

Note to A Grandparent

By writing your direct answers to the questions asked here, you will create a lasting story of yourself and your family. Please take your time in answering these questions. Try to include as many dates as you can. If some questions are not applicable, skip them or cross them out and use the space for other information and memories you would like to record. You may prefer to draft your answer on scrap paper before entering it onto these pages. And don't forget to sign your name on the first page!

It is hoped that this book will give you the double pleasure of completing a work of creative expression, and giving your grandchild a most personal and unique gift to treasure forever.

Beginnings

Beginnings

Where were you when I was born?

_____

Did you predict correctly
whether I would be a boy or girl?

_____

_____

How did you find out I had arrived?

_____

_____

_____

Who were the first people you told?

_____

_____

Did you suggest a name,
or names, for me?

_____

When and where was the first time
you saw me?

_____

Notes:

Beginnings

Where were you born?
(City or town, state, country)

_____

_____

What was the month, day and year?
What time was it?

_____

_____

How much did you weigh at birth?
Were you a healthy new-born baby?

_____

_____

What were your parents' names?
How old were they?

_____

_____

_____

_____

Notes:

Beginnings

Was there anything unusual about the circumstances of your birth?

What was your full name?

Does your name have a special meaning?

Notes:

When You Were Very Young

When You Were Very Young

Where is the first home you remember?
    What did it look like?

_____

_____

_____

Who were your neighbors?

_____

_____

_____

Who was your first "best friend"?

_____

_____

Who were your other friends?

_____

_____

Do you still have any favorite things
    that you had as a child?

_____

_____

_____

Notes:

When You Were Very Young

Did you have brothers/sisters when
*   you were very young? When were they born?*

_____

_____

What do you remember about your
*   room?*

_____

_____

What were your favorite toys?

_____

_____

What were your favorite games?

_____

_____

What is the first present
*   you remember giving? To Whom?*

_____

_____

Notes:

When You Were Very Young

What is the first present you remember receiving?

_____

_____

_____

What was your favorite book?

_____

_____

_____

Did you have favorite stories?

_____

_____

_____

Did you have a secret hiding place?

_____

_____

_____

Notes:

When You Were Very Young

Did your family have any pets?

What kind?

What were their names?

Did you have favorite relatives?

Did you have a nickname?

How did you get it?

Did you like or dislike it?

Notes:

When You Were Very Young

Who took care of you if your
parents were away?

_____

_____

_____

_____

Did you have a grown-up friend
who was not a relative?

_____

_____

_____

_____

What was the first movie you saw?

_____

_____

_____

_____

Notes:

When You Were Very Young

What were your favorite radio programs?

_____

_____

_____

What were your favorite TV programs?

_____

_____

_____

What indoor games did you play?

_____

_____

What outdoor games did you play?

_____

_____

Who did you play with?

_____

_____

_____

Notes:

When You Were Very Young

Is there one special early memory
*   you have of your mother?*

_____

_____

_____

_____

_____

_____

Is there one special early memory
*   you have of your father?*

_____

_____

_____

_____

_____

_____

Notes:

Growing Up

Growing Up: Grammar School Years

What grammar school did you go to?
Where was it?

When did you attend?

Who were your favorite teachers?
What was special about them?

What were your favorite
grammar school subjects?

Were you in any school plays
or concerts?

What did you do after school?

Notes:

Growing Up: Grammar School Years

*Who were your best friends
  in grammar school?*

_____

_____

_____

*How late did you stay up during
  school nights?*

_____

_____

_____

What chores did you have at home?

_____

_____

_____

_____

_____

Notes:

Growing Up: Grammar School Years

*What do you remember about
    your summer vacations?*

*What do you remember about
    the school buildings?*

Did you get an allowance?

How did you spend it?

Notes:

Growing Up: High School Years

What high school did you go to?
Where was it?

_____

_____

Who were your favorite high school teachers?
What was special about them?

_____

_____

_____

Who were the teachers you didn't
like? What do you remember about them?

_____

_____

What were your favorite
high school subjects?

_____

_____

_____

Notes:

Growing Up: High School Years

What subjects did you dislike?

_____

_____

_____

Who were your closest friends?

_____

_____

_____

What were your favorite sports?

_____

_____

_____

_____

Were you on any school teams?

_____

_____

_____

_____

Notes:

Growing Up: High School Years

Did you belong to any clubs?
What were they?

_____

_____

_____

Were you involved in any activities
—i.e. newspaper, scholastic clubs, etc.?

_____

_____

_____

Did you win any academic, social
or athletic awards or prizes?

_____

_____

_____

_____

Who was the most envied person
in your school? Why?

_____

_____

_____

_____

Notes:

Growing Up: High School Years

What teacher influenced you the most?

_____

_____

_____

Who did you date?

_____

_____

_____

Was there someone you wanted to
*   date but never did?*

_____

_____

_____

What did you want to be or do when
*   you were finished with high school?*

_____

_____

_____

Notes:

Growing Up: High School Years

What friends had the most influence
on you?

_____

_____

_____

Did you fight with anyone? Who was
it and what did you fight over?

_____

_____

_____

Did you have any part-time jobs
during the school year?

_____

_____

_____

How much money did you earn?

_____

_____

_____

Notes:

Growing Up: High School Years

What did you like best about
summer vacations?

Did you ever work during summer
vacations? What did you do?

How much did you earn?

What were your favorite books?

What were your favorite movies?

Notes:

Growing Up: High School Years

Who were your favorite athletes?

_____

_____

_____

What magazines did you read?

_____

_____

_____

What television or radio programs did
you follow?

_____

_____

Who were your favorite actors or
actresses?

_____

_____

_____

Notes:

Growing Up: High School Years

What were the most popular songs?

_____

_____

_____

_____

What dances did you do?

_____

_____

_____

What were your favorite clothes?

_____

_____

_____

What were the major clothing fads?

_____

_____

_____

Notes:

Growing Up: High School Years

*What were the most popular slang
    terms and phrases?*

_____

_____

_____

*What did you do in high school that
    gave you the most satisfaction?*

_____

_____

_____

*What was the greatest disappointment
    you experienced?*

_____

_____

Did you drive a car?

_____

_____

Notes:

Growing Up: High School Years

Who taught you how to drive?

_____

_____

_____

What kind of car did you drive?

_____

_____

*How did you get along with
     your mother?*

_____

_____

_____

*How did you get along with
     your father?*

_____

_____

_____

Notes:

Growing Up: High School Years

*Who were the adults you considered
    friends?*

What were your neighbors like?

Who did you have "crushes" on?

Did you fall in love with anyone?

Notes:

Growing Up: College, University Years

Did you go to college?
Where was it?

_____

_____

What was your major course of study?

_____

_____

Did you have any outstanding or
memorable teachers?

_____

_____

_____

What were your goals when you were
a student?

_____

_____

_____

Were you involved in any extra-
curricular activities?

_____

_____

_____

_____

Notes:

Growing Up: College, University Years

Were you a member of any clubs?

*What were your most important
learning experiences?*

What kind of a student were you?

*Did you receive any awards,
prizes, or degrees?*

What do you remember best?

Notes:

Growing Up: College, University Years

*Did you attend any graduate
   or professional schools? Why?*

What did you study?

*Did you receive any awards,
   prizes, or degrees?*

*Who were your closest
   friends and roommates?*

What do you remember best?

Notes:

Friends

Friends

*What friends have you stayed in touch
with since childhood?*

*What friends have you stayed in touch
with since your teen years?*

*What friends have surprised you by
getting in touch?*

*What friends have you meant to keep
in touch with, but haven't?*

What friendships have you renewed?

Notes:

Friends

Who are your closest friends now?
How did you meet them?

_____

_____

_____

What recent acquaintances have
become friends?

_____

_____

_____

Have you ever gone to a reunion? Which?
What was it like? How did you react?

_____

_____

_____

_____

Notes:

Friends

Do you have any friends who became famous?

*What is the strangest place you ever
    began a friendship?*

Who is your most amusing friend?

*Have you ever had a serious quarrel
    with a friend? What happened?*

Notes:

Friends

Where and when did you meet your
  husband's/wife's best friend?

_____

_____

_____

What is your favorite story about
  any of your friends?

_____

_____

_____

_____

_____

Who, within the family, has been your
  best friend?

_____

_____

_____

Notes:

Friends

*What friends have done, or would do,
    the most for you without being asked?*

_____

_____

_____

*Have you done things for friends with-
    out them knowing it? What? When?*

_____

_____

_____

What do you most value in a friendship?

_____

_____

_____

Who is the best friend you've ever had?

_____

_____

_____

Notes:

At Your
Own Home

At Your Own Home

When did you leave your parents' home?
   Why and where did you move?

_____

_____

_____

How much rent did you pay?

_____

What did your home look like?
   How large was it? How was it furnished?

_____

_____

_____

_____

_____

How long did you live there?
   Why did you next move? Where?

_____

_____

_____

Notes:

At Your Own Home

*How many other houses or apartments
     have you lived in?*

*What were your addresses? When were
     you there?*

*Do you have any furnishings that
     belonged to your parents?*

Notes:

At Your Own Home

What is the least expensive home or
apartment you've ever had?

_____

_____

_____

What is the most expensive?

_____

_____

_____

Which homes or apartments have you
enjoyed the most? Why?

_____

_____

_____

_____

_____

_____

_____

_____

Notes:

At Your Own Home

*What room have you liked the best
in any of your homes?*

_____

_____

_____

_____

_____

*What have been your favorite pieces
of furniture?*

_____

_____

_____

_____

_____

_____

Notes:

At Your Own Home

*Who have been your favorite
    neighbors?*

_____

_____

_____

_____

_____

*Who have been the most irritating
    neighbors?*

_____

_____

_____

_____

_____

_____

Notes:

Marriage

Marriage

How did you meet my grandfather/
grandmother?

How old were you?
How old was he/she?

What attracted you to each other?

How long did you know each other
before you discussed marriage?

How did you become engaged?

Notes:

Marriage

*How did your parents react when
   you told them?*

_____

_____

*How did his/her parents react when
   you told them?*

_____

_____

_____

*What do you remember most about
   your courtship?*

_____

_____

_____

*What ring or token did you give or
   receive as an engagement present?*

_____

_____

Notes:

Marriage

When and where were you married?

_____

_____

What did you wear?

_____

_____

_____

Who was at your wedding?

_____

_____

_____

_____

*What do you remember best about the
    ceremony?*

_____

_____

_____

_____

Notes:

Marriage

*Where did you spend the first night
of your marriage?*

_____

_____

*Did you receive wedding presents?
What were they?*

_____

_____

*Do you have photographs of your
wedding? Where are they?*

_____

_____

_____

_____

*Did you go on a honeymoon? Where?
How long?*

_____

_____

Notes:

Marriage

*What were the first things you
    bought together for your home?*

_____

_____

_____

*What surprised you most about my
    grandfather/grandmother after you married?*

_____

_____

_____

*What was the first argument you had
    after the wedding?*

_____

_____

_____

_____

Notes:

Marriage

*What friends have you seen most as
a couple?*

_____

_____

*What has he/she done that has made
you proud?*

_____

_____

*What pastimes, games, sports or
leisure interests do you share?*

_____

_____

*Have you and your husband/wife enjoyed
good health? If not, what were the problems?*

_____

_____

_____

_____

Notes:

Marriage

What is your favorite story about
*   my grandmother/grandfather?*

_____

_____

_____

_____

_____

_____

_____

_____

_____

_____

_____

Did you marry more than once?
*   Whom?*

_____

_____

Did you have children by another
*   marriage?*

_____

_____

Notes:

Travel

A Grandparents Book

Travel

How old were you when you took your first trip?
   Where did you go? How did you travel?

Which childhood trip do you remember
   most vividly? Why?

When did you take your first plane
   ride? Were you scared?

Did you or your parents take photographs of your
   trips? Do you still have any?

Notes:

Travel

Do you remember the first hotel
you stayed in? Which one? When?

_____

_____

_____

What is the most adventurous thing
that occurred while you were travelling?

_____

_____

_____

_____

_____

What is the funniest thing that ever
happened to you during a trip?

_____

_____

_____

_____

Notes:

Travel

Were you ever lost while travelling?

_____

_____

_____

*Were you ever in need of a Good Sam-
    aritan on a trip? Did you find one?*

_____

_____

_____

Have you had any health problems while travelling?

_____

_____

_____

*Where did you go on your first trip
    with your husband/wife?*

_____

_____

_____

Notes:

Travel

*What is the most exotic or extra-
ordinary trip you've taken?*

_____

_____

_____

_____

_____

_____

_____

_____

*What is the strangest mode of trans-
portation you've used while on a trip?*

_____

_____

_____

_____

Notes:

Travel

*What is the best trip the two of you
have taken together?*

_____

_____

_____

_____

_____

_____

*Do you have any purchases or mementos
from your travels?*

_____

_____

_____

_____

_____

_____

Notes:

Travel

Have you ever travelled with friends?
When? With whom? Where did you go?

_____

_____

Have you made any friends while trav-
elling? When and how?

_____

_____

_____

_____

What foreign countries have you
travelled to?

_____

_____

_____

_____

_____

Notes:

Travel

What places would you return to?

_____

_____

_____

_____

What places would you not return to?

_____

_____

_____

Have you ever taken a cruise?
      What ship? How long was the trip?

_____

_____

_____

_____

Notes:

Travel

What is the best hotel you stayed in? Why?

_____

_____

_____

_____

_____

What is the best restaurant you've eaten in while travelling?

_____

_____

_____

_____

_____

_____

Notes:

Travel

*What is the most spectacular sight
you've seen while travelling?*

_____

_____

_____

_____

*What is the single greatest memory
you have of a trip you've taken?*

_____

_____

_____

_____

_____

_____

_____

Notes:

Work, Jobs, Money

Work, Jobs, Money

*What was your first full-time job? How much did you
    earn? What were your responsibilities?*

_____

_____

_____

_____

Describe your first boss.

_____

_____

_____

*What has been your main occupation? Why did you
    choose it? How did you get started?*

_____

_____

_____

For whom have you worked?

_____

_____

_____

_____

Notes:

Work, Jobs, Money

What other jobs have you had?

_____

_____

_____

_____

What is the most important promotion
you've received?

_____

_____

_____

What was the most difficult job
you've done?

_____

_____

_____

_____

Notes:

Work, Jobs, Money

Have you ever owned your own business?

How did it start?

Who or what has been the most important help to you in your work?

Notes:

Work, Jobs, Money

What is the most extravagant
thing you've ever done?

_____

_____

_____

_____

_____

_____

_____

Have you ever been caught in a
severe financial crisis?

_____

_____

_____

_____

_____

_____

Notes:

Work, Jobs, Money

*What do you think is the soundest
     investment one can make?*

Notes:

Family Lore

Family Lore

What were your grandparents' names?

Where did they come from?
    What did they do?

What memories do you have of them?

Who were your great aunts and uncles?
    Where did they live?

What did they do? What memories
    do you have of them?

Notes:

Family Lore

What were/are your parents' names?

_____

_____

Where did/do they live?

_____

_____

What did/do they do?

_____

_____

What are your memories of the home
you grew up in?

_____

_____

_____

_____

Notes:

Family Lore

*What are your thoughts about
your mother?*

_____

_____

*What are your thoughts about
your father?*

_____

_____

*What are the most important things
you have learned from your father?*

_____

_____

_____

*What are the most important things
you have learned from your mother?*

_____

_____

_____

Notes:

Family Lore

Do you have aunts and uncles?

What special thoughts do you have of them?

Do you have brothers and sisters?
  How did/do you get along with them?

What did they look like when they
  were teenagers?

Notes:

Family Lore

What work have they done?

_____

_____

_____

Where are they now?

_____

_____

*How far back can you trace your
    mother's family?*

_____

_____

_____

*How far back can you trace your
    father's family?*

_____

_____

_____

Notes:

Family Lore

Do we have any famous relatives?
Who? What have they done?

_____

_____

_____

Who do you feel are our most successful
relatives? What have they accomplished?

_____

_____

_____

Are there any characteristics which
you feel run through the family?

_____

_____

_____

_____

Do you look more like your mother
or your father?

_____

_____

_____

_____

Notes:

Family Lore

Are there specific first names that
are repeated through the family?

_____

_____

_____

Have members of the family followed
similar occupations or professions?

_____

_____

Have there been any exceptional athletes
in the family?

_____

_____

_____

Which relatives possess artistic talents?
What?

_____

_____

Are there any medical problems
that seem to run in the family?

_____

_____

_____

Notes:

Family Lore

Do we have any family legends?

_____

_____

_____

What family traditions have we
  always followed?

_____

_____

Are there any family "black sheep"?
  Who are they? What did they do?

_____

_____

_____

Are there any curios or mementoes that
  have been handed down over the years?

_____

_____

_____

Notes:

Family Lore

*Are there any family photographs or
records? Where are they now?*

_____

_____

*Are there any favorite stories that
are told and retold?*

_____

_____

_____

_____

_____

*Who was the most beautiful woman
in the family?*

_____

*Who was the most handsome man
in the family?*

_____

Notes:

Religion

Religion

Do you believe in God?

_____

_____

_____

Do you regularly attend a house of
worship? Which one?

_____

_____

_____

Who is the first member of the clergy you
recall? What was he like?

_____

_____

Has a member of the clergy had an
influence on you? How?

_____

_____

_____

Did you attend a religious school?
Which one? When?

_____

_____

_____

Notes:

Religion

Did you ever want to become a
member of the clergy?

_____

_____

_____

What is your favorite prayer?

_____

_____

_____

_____

What is your favorite religious music?

_____

_____

Are you active in social activities
(choral, fund raising, etc.) in your house of worship?

_____

_____

_____

Notes:

Religion

Is religion a major factor in your life?

_____

_____

_____

How often do you read the Bible?
What is your favorite passage?

_____

_____

_____

_____

Do you interpret the Bible strictly
or loosely?

_____

_____

_____

Notes:

Religion

Have you ever explored other
*   religions? Which ones? How?*

_____

_____

What was your most important
*   religious experience?*

_____

_____

_____

Have you conducted any religious
*   ceremonies in your home? What and when?*

_____

_____

What religious rituals or historic
*   figures are most important to you?*

_____

_____

_____

Notes:

Religion

*How much religious training did you
   receive from your parents?*

_____

_____

*How much religious training did you
   give your children?*

_____

_____

*Have there been times when you
   questioned your religion? When and how?*

_____

_____

_____

*How do you feel about prayers in
   schools?*

_____

_____

_____

Notes:

Religion

*Have there been times when your
    religion has helped you through difficult personal moments?*

When?

What happened?

*How do you feel about children
    being taught by members of religious orders?*

Notes:

Religion

*At what period in your life has
    religion been most important to you?*

_____

_____

_____

_____

_____

_____

*Do you remember any bedtime prayers
    you said as a child? What were they?*

_____

_____

_____

_____

_____

Notes:

Some Favorite Things

A Grandparents Book

Some Favorite Things

What are your favorite foods?

Drinks?

Animals?

Colors?

Places in the world?

Flowers?

Gifts to give?

Notes:

Some Favorite Things

Gifts to receive?

Times of day?

Painting?

Sculpture?

Age?

Season?

Building?

Notes:

Some Favorite Things

Magazines/Newspapers?

Authors?

Journalists?

Commentators?

Books?

Singers/Groups?

Orchestras/Bands?

Notes:

Some Favorite Things

Operas?

Symphonies?

Ballets?

Dances?

TV actors/actresses?

Notes:

Some Favorite Things

TV shows?

_____

_____

_____

Film actors/actresses?

_____

_____

_____

Films?

_____

_____

_____

Musicians?

_____

_____

_____

Notes:

Some Favorite Things

Radio programs?

Comedians?

Comic strips?

Painters/Illustrators?

Notes:

Some Favorite Things

Athletes?

_____

_____

_____

Spectator sports?

_____

_____

_____

Participant sports?

_____

_____

_____

Sayings?

_____

_____

_____

_____

Notes:

Holidays and Traditions

Holidays and Traditions

What is your favorite holiday?
What memories does it bring back?

_____

_____

_____

How do you observe it?

_____

_____

_____

What do you consider the most important
family holidays?

_____

_____

Which family members have been
responsible for hosting various holidays?

_____

_____

_____

Are there any traditional family foods?

_____

_____

_____

Notes:

Holidays and Traditions

Are there any traditional family
toasts?

Have you ever observed holidays of
religions other than yours?

With whom?
Where?

Notes:

Holidays and Traditions

*What birthdays of family members
    have been important celebrations?*

_____

_____

_____

What have been your best birthday parties?

_____

_____

_____

*What are the best gifts you've
    ever received?*

_____

_____

_____

_____

Notes:

Holidays and Traditions

*Did anyone ever have a surprise
    party for you?*

   *What happened?
   Were you really surprised?*

_____

_____

_____

_____

*What have been your most memorable
    wedding anniversaries?*

_____

_____

_____

_____

_____

_____

Notes:

Holidays and Traditions

Did your family gather together frequently?
Or just for the holidays?

_____

_____

_____

What holiday traditions do you hope
I give to my own children?

_____

_____

_____

_____

_____

_____

_____

_____

_____

Notes:

Pastimes,
Hobbies,
Collections

Pastimes, Hobbies, Collections

What do you most enjoy doing?

_____

_____

What talents or abilities have you
tried to develop?

_____

_____

Have you ever been on a stage?
What happened?

_____

_____

Have you ever had your name in a
newspaper? What paper? When and why?

_____

_____

_____

Have you ever been on television?
When and why?

_____

_____

_____

What type of books do you read most
often?

_____

_____

Notes:

Pastimes, Hobbies, Collections

Have you ever won a drawing or a
lottery? What did you win?

_____

_____

Have you gambled or made bets?

_____

What have you bet on?

_____

_____

_____

Do you play cards? What are your
favorite card games?

_____

_____

_____

Who are your favorite card partners?

_____

_____

_____

_____

Notes:

Pastimes, Hobbies, Collections

Have you played musical instruments?
Which ones?

How did you learn?
How long did you practice?

What music did you play?

Notes:

Pastimes, Hobbies, Collections

Have you collected things?

    Stamps?

    Coins?

    Antiques?

    Art?

    Models?

Notes:

Pastimes, Hobbies, Collections

Recipes?

Toys?

Books?

Records?

Other collectibles?

Where are your collections now?

Notes:

Pastimes, Hobbies, Collections

Have you had other hobbies?

What organizations, clubs, or associations
  do you or have you belonged to?

What did they do?

How active have you been?

Notes:

Pastimes, Hobbies, Collections

Have you been active in any charities
  as a volunteer?

What did you do?

What are your other interests?

Notes:

My Parent
Your Child

My Parent/Your Child

When and where was my mother/father born?
How big was she/he?

_____

_____

Who delivered the baby?

_____

_____

Who was present?

_____

_____

Who were the first people you told?

_____

_____

How did you choose the name?

_____

_____

What was my parent like when she/
he was a small child?

_____

_____

_____

_____

Notes:

My Parent/Your Child

What were the first words my parent ever spoke?

At what age did my parent take his/ her first steps?

Were you a firm or easy-going parent? How did he/she react?

Notes:

My Parent/Your Child

What was his/her favorite entertainment
as a teenager?

_____

_____

_____

_____

_____

_____

What did my mother/father want to
be when she/he grew up?

_____

_____

_____

_____

_____

Notes:

My Parent/Your Child

*What did you think she/he would
    grow up to become?*

_____

_____

_____

What did she/he look like?

_____

_____

_____

*What did she /he do that made you
    angry?*

_____

_____

*What did she/he do that made you
    proud?*

_____

_____

_____

Notes:

My Parent/Your Child

How was she/he as a student?

_____

_____

_____

What clothes did she/he wear?

_____

_____

_____

Did she/he ever get into trouble?

_____

_____

_____

What chores did you make her/him do?

_____

_____

_____

_____

Notes:

My Parent/Your Child

How much was her/his allowance?

_____

_____

_____

Did she/he have a nickname?
      How did she/he get it?

_____

_____

_____

What were her/his special talents?

_____

_____

_____

What were her/his best habits?

_____

_____

_____

Notes:

My Parent/Your Child

What were her/his bad habits?

_____

_____

_____

_____

Did she/he have a pet?

_____

_____

_____

_____

What did she/he want badly that you
gave her/him?

_____

_____

_____

_____

What did she/he talk about?

_____

_____

_____

_____

_____

Notes:

My Parent/Your Child

*What were the most difficult
   questions she/he asked?*

_____

_____

_____

_____

Who in the family did she/he resemble?

_____

_____

_____

*What did you find most difficult
   to allow her/him to do?*

_____

_____

_____

*How did you meet your future son/
   daughter-in-law (my father/mother)?*

_____

_____

_____

Notes:

My Parent/Your Child

What did you think?

_____

_____

_____

What did you have to say?

_____

_____

_____

_____

Did you feel they would get married?

_____

_____

Tell me about my parents' wedding.

_____

_____

_____

_____

_____

Notes:

History
and
Politics

History and Politics

To which political party do you belong? Why?

_____

_____

_____

Which national candidates have you
voted for over the years?

_____

_____

_____

Which local candidates have you
backed over the years?

_____

_____

_____

Have you worked in a political campaign?
For Whom?

When?
What did you do?

_____

_____

Notes:

History and Politics

What do you feel government does well?

_____

_____

_____

_____

_____

_____

What do you feel government does badly?

_____

_____

_____

_____

_____

_____

Notes:

History and Politics

*What is your most vivid **historical memory**?*

_____

_____

_____

_____

*What world events have most affected
    your life?*

_____

_____

_____

*What inventions or technological advances **have**
    most changed your life? How?*

_____

_____

_____

_____

Notes:

History and Politics

*What national events have most
    affected your life?*

_____

_____

_____

_____

_____

*What local events have affected
    your life?*

_____

_____

_____

_____

_____

_____

Notes:

History and Politics

*What causes or issues do you now feel
    strongly about?*

*What causes or issues have you felt
    strongly about in the past?*

Notes:

Between Us

Between Us

What are you most proud of doing?

_____

_____

_____

_____

_____

What are you most proud of being?

_____

_____

_____

_____

_____

_____

_____

Notes:

Between Us

*Have you ever gone to a psychiatrist
or a psychologist?*

What do you think about therapy?

What do you think about using them?

What was your most exciting experience?

Notes:

Between Us

What was your happiest experience?

_____

_____

_____

_____

_____

_____

What was your saddest experience?

_____

_____

_____

_____

_____

Notes:

Between Us

What goals have you set for your future?

_____

_____

_____

_____

_____

What do you hope the future holds for me?

_____

_____

_____

_____

_____

Notes:

Between Us

Who do you love? What do you love?

_____

_____

_____

_____

_____

_____

_____

_____

_____

_____

_____

_____

Notes:

Memorabilia

Photographs, Clippings, Cards, Letters

Memorabilia

Photographs, Clippings, Cards, Letters

Memorabilia

Photographs, Clippings, Cards, Letters

Memorabilia

Photographs, Clippings, Cards, Letters

Memorabilia

Photographs, Clippings, Cards, Letters

Memorabilia

Photographs, Clippings, Cards, Letters

Memorabilia

Photographs, Clippings, Cards, Letters

Memorabilia

Photographs, Clippings, Cards, Letters

A
Grandparents
Book